# GIFTWRAP,
# BOXES & CARDS

# Easy TO MAKE

# GIFTWRAP, BOXES & CARDS

## KERRIE DUDLEY

ANAYA PUBLISHERS LTD LONDON

First published in Great Britain in 1994
by Anaya Publishers Ltd, Strode House,
44–50 Osnaburgh Street, London NW1 3ND

**Editor** Helen Douglas-Cooper
**Design** Watermark Communications Group Ltd
**Photography** Steve Tanner
**Illustrations** Stephen Dew

British Library in Publication Data

Dudley, Kerrie
Easy to Make Giftwrap, Boxes and Cards.
(Easy to Make Series)
I. Title   II. Series
745.5
ISBN 1 85470 196 7

Typeset by Servis Filmsetting Ltd, Manchester, UK.
Colour Reproduction by HBM Print Pte Ltd, Singapore.
Produced by Mandarin Offset
Printed and bound in Hong Kong.

# CONTENTS

# Introduction

*Giving cards and presents is an all-year-round activity. Here are ideas for hand-made cards and boxes to give your gifts and greetings a personal touch.*

The custom of exchanging gifts to mark special occasions goes back many centuries. The imperial Romans gave small gifts to their friends at the beginning of the year as a token of good health. The wise men brought gifts to the holy baby in Bethlehem almost 2,000 years ago. And in Japan, the art of wrapping a gift has always been part of the spiritual and cultural life.

The sending or exchanging of greetings cards has a shorter history. The earliest Valentines, messages of love often written on a piece of flat card, were exchanged in the middle of the eighteenth century, but it was almost another 100 years before the first Christmas cards were published. Today, throughout the world, greetings cards for every imaginable occasion are sent.

Although a wide variety of cards are commercially available, there are many arguments for making your own. I think the most important is that a hand-made card, however simple, is unique and will make the recipient feel special. They will know that time and effort has been expended on their behalf, and they will possibly treasure the card for ever. A hand-made card also gives pleasure to you, the maker. It is very satisfying to produce something imaginative with your own hands. Commercial cards, especially those with character, are becoming very expensive, so it is also often cheaper to produce your own.

Gift boxes, too, are expensive and often not available in the size, shape or colour you want. A hand-made box or giftwrap can be as imaginative and attractive as the present it conceals.

This book provides ideas for both, and is divided into two main chapters, 'Giftwrapping with style' and 'Greetings for every occasion'.

## Giftwrapping with style

Giftwrapping not only protects the contents, it also initially conceals the gift from the recipient so that there is an element of surprise on opening it. A beautifully wrapped parcel shows, too, that the gift has been chosen with care.

This chapter shows you how to make a number of boxes, including a heart-shaped box, a square box and a hexagonal box. From those shown, boxes in almost any other shape can be made and decorated to suit the occasion. It also shows how to make tote bags and pyramid plant holders, as well as ways to wrap with fabric and methods of making your own giftwrap using marbling and paste paper.

Some projects demonstrate how to use different techniques to decorate the parcel. These include assorted ways with ribbons and bows, paper appliqué and relief cutting, making paper flowers, rubber stamping and card collage.

You will also find more wrapping methods in the final chapter 'Better techniques', which also explains how to make decorative cord and provides ideas for gift tags and envelopes.

## Greetings for all occasions

This chapter shows how to make a number of different kinds of cards. Although many are designed for specific dates and events, they can be adapted to suit most occasions.

Making cards is an excellent way to try out a new craft. The result can be seen quickly and, as it is worked on a small scale, mistakes are not too costly. Several crafts are included that you may not have tried before – perhaps quilling, making paper lace, or embroidery on perforated paper. All designs are kept fairly simple to give you a taste of the craft. Then, if you enjoy it, you can go on to design your own cards.

Some of the designs will also delight youngsters – an Easter bunny that wobbles on a spring and a Christmas angel that rocks. With adult help, especially when using scissors or spray adhesive, children will enjoy joining in with most of the projects. However, some of the techniques, especially the use of craft knives, should be reserved for adults. You will find useful tips on the use of tools and adhesives in the final chapter, 'Better techniques'. With care, making your own giftwrap and greetings cards can be very enjoyable.

# Gift wrapping

# Heart box

*Whether for Valentine's Day or another romantic occasion, this gift box is ideal for someone you love. The method can be adapted for any shape of box with a lid.*

## Materials
Squared paper
Thick card (for base and lid)
Spray adhesive
Thin card (for the sides)
Contact glue
Silver paper
Giftwrap
30in (76cm) of ribbon for bow
Double-sided sticky tape

## Preparation
1 Decide on the size of the box and enlarge the heart pattern on to squared paper and cut out. Use this to cut out 2 hearts in thick card. Stick the 2 pieces together with spray adhesive.

2 Measure around the edge of the heart with a tape measure and add 1in (2.5cm). Cut out a strip of thin card to this length; the width should equal the required depth of the box.

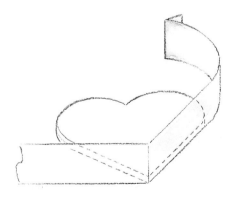

Stick the strip of card round one side of the heart at a time

## Working the design
3 To make the base of the box fold the strip of card in half, cut ½in (12mm) from one end, and fold back ½in (12mm) at the other end. Spread contact glue around the edge of the card heart and place it flat on the work surface with the point towards you. Starting at the point of the heart and at the fold halfway along the strip of card, apply the strip round the heart, working around one side at a time and ensuring that the strip is vertical. Stick down the overlap at the top of the heart.

4 Place the base down on the back of a piece of silver paper and draw round it. Cut out the shape allowing ½in (12mm) extra all round. Cut notches into this margin up to the drawn line. Lay it flat, wrong side up, and spray with adhesive. Press the base of the box down on to it, lining up the base with the drawn line. Fold the tabs up around the sides and stick down.

5 Cut a strip of giftwrap ½in (12mm) longer than the circumference of the box and ½in (12mm) wider than the depth. Spray the back with adhesive and stick to the sides of the box, lining up the bottom edge of the giftwrap just above the bottom of the box. Snip the overlap around the top in several places. Fold the tabs over and stick to the inside of the base.

6 For the lid, place the base on a piece of thick card and draw round it. Cut out 2 hearts. Stick the 2 pieces together.
   For the sides of the lid, measure and cut a strip of thin card and stick it

Enlarge the heart on squared paper to use as a template

around the edge, as for the base. Cut a strip of silver paper 1in (2.5cm) wider than the depth of the lid. Cut notches $\frac{1}{2}$in (12mm) deep along both long edges. Spray the back with adhesive and stick the strip around the sides of the lid. Stick down one notched edge on the top of the lid and the other to the inside.

**7** Draw around the lid on to the back of a piece of giftwrap. Cut it out about $\frac{1}{8}$in (3mm) smaller all around. Spray the back and stick it to the top of the lid. Cut a strip of giftwrap $\frac{1}{4}$in (6mm) narrower than the depth of the lid. Stick it around the sides.

**8** For the bow, stick a piece of double-sided sticky tape to one end of the piece of ribbon. Make the centre loop with this end and stick together with the tape. Stick a small piece of tape to the back of this loop and make another loop to one side, sticking in place. Repeat on the other side. Then repeat on alternate sides until the ribbon is used up. Stick the bow to the box with double-sided sticky tape.

# Paper prints

*Decorating your own paper is an easy way to produce inexpensive and attractive giftwrap. Experiment with different designs and colours to suit the occasion.*

**Materials**
**For both types of giftwrap:**
Wallpaper paste
Sheets of paper

**For the marbled giftwrap:**
Artists' oil paints in 1 or 2 colours
White spirit

**For the paste paper:**
Watercolour paints in 1 or 2 colours
Pieces of sponge
Pieces of card

## MARBLED PAPER
### Preparation
1 Make a very weak solution of wallpaper paste (size) using 1 heaped tablespoon to 2pt (1 litre) of water in a large tray (such as a roasting tin).

2 Mix the paints separately with white spirit to quite a thin dropping consistency. Test its consistency by dripping some paint into the tray of wallpaper paste. It should spread in its immediate area. If it does not spread, it is too thick; if it disperses over a wide area, it is too thin. The paint can be cleared off the surface of the size by dragging strips of newspaper or absorbent kitchen paper across it.

3 Cut sheets of paper slightly smaller than the tin.

### Working the design
4 Drip the paint on to the size. Use a drinking straw or cocktail stick to make patterns with the paint.

5 Carefully lower a sheet of paper on to the surface, making sure that no air bubbles are trapped under it. Then, holding the paper by 2 adjacent corners, lift it off the surface and allow the size to drip off. Lay the paper pattern side up on newspaper to dry.

## PASTE PAPER
### Preparation
1 Mix the wallpaper paste according to the instructions on the packet. Divide it into separate containers according to the number of different colours you want to use. Add watercolour paint and mix well. Add more paint if necessary.

### Working the design
2 Spread the coloured paste mixtures on to a sheet of paper using a large brush.

3 Make patterns in the paste with a piece of card cut into a comb, or a piece of sponge. If you don't like the result, brush over with more paste and start again.

4 Lay the paper on newspaper to dry.

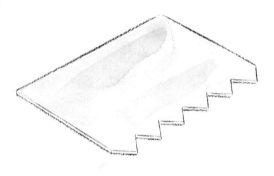

Make a card comb

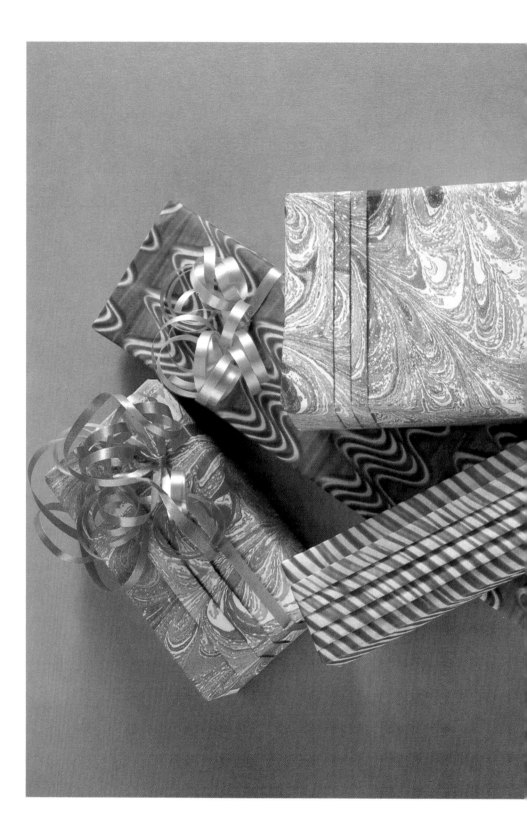

## Curl clusters

Tie a narrow strip of synthetic gift ribbon around the parcel and knot it on top. Tie 3 or 4 strips of at least 12in (30cm) long to the knot so that you have 6 or 8 half lengths. Hold a piece near the knot between your thumb and the blade of a pair of scissors. To curl the ribbon, pull the blade rapidly along the length of the ribbon.

# Hexagon box

*The floral-shaped top of this box is made by overlapping one flap on top of the next. The folds are easier to make with a fairly large box, using thin card.*

**Materials**

Thin card, differently coloured on each
  side (it is better to buy this than make
  your own)
Pair of compasses
Decorative paper ribbon
Stick adhesive

**Preparation**

**1** Following the diagram, draw the
measurements for the size of box you
need on a sheet of card, with the colour
to go on the outside of the box facing you.
The height of the top section should be
twice the width of a side section (A), and
A should measure at least 2½in (6.5cm).

**2** To draw the base section accurately,
use a pair of compasses. Set the radius to
equal A. Place the point on each mark B
in turn and draw intersecting arcs on
each base flap. Draw the shape of the
flaps as shown.

**3** To draw the scalloped top, find point
C, which is equal to half A from the top
edge. Then set the radius of the
compasses to half A, place the point of
the compass on each point C in turn and
draw a semi-circle.

**4** Cut out the box, including the base
flaps, but do not cut out the scallops at
this stage.

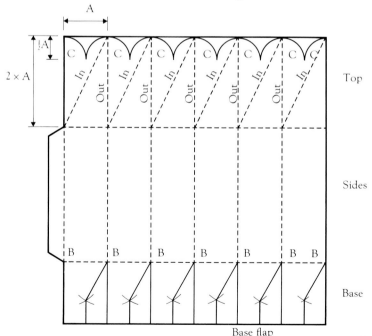

Draw the dimensions of the box on a sheet of
thin card

– – Score and fold

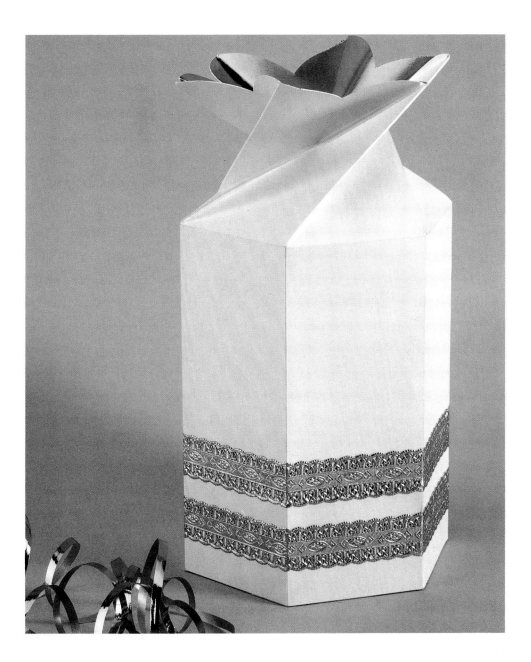

**Working the design**
**5** Starting with the vertical lines, score along the fold lines and then crease along them to create the shape of the box. Repeat along the horizontal lines. Score the diagonal lines and crease each one, starting at the left-hand side, at the same time folding each flap over the next. Open out the box. Cut out the scallops.

**6** The box will be easier to open and close if the side and base flaps are left unstuck and are just tucked in. The base flaps are tucked inside so that just the diagonal edges show.

**Finishing**
**7** Decorate the box with braid, ribbon or strips of gift wrap.

# Tote bags

*Tote bags are ideal for awkwardly shaped gifts. They can be made from a sheet of giftwrap, but for heavier items laminate the giftwrap to stronger paper or card.*

## Materials
Decorative paper
Cartridge paper (optional)
Spray adhesive
Thin card
Stick adhesive
Cord or ribbon for handles

## Preparation
**1** Adapt the basic pattern to the size of bag you wish to make. All 'A' measurements should be equal and the depth of the base overlap (marked $A + \frac{1}{2}$) should measure approximately $1\frac{1}{2}$ times the depth of the sides.

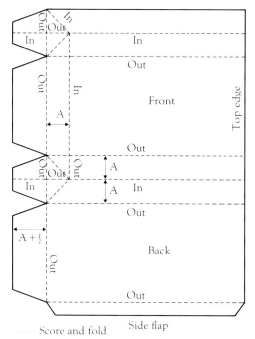

Mark the dimensions of the bag on a piece of paper

**2** Following the diagram, draw the measurements on to a sheet of cartridge paper. Cut out. Starting with the main vertical lines, crease the fold lines to shape. Crease the base line and the fold line that runs across the front section. Carefully crease the triangular-shaped sections. Next, fold the side lines together, and pinch the triangles into place. Open out again.

## Working the design
**3** Lay the paper flat, creased side up, and spray with adhesive. Lay the decorative paper flat, wrong side up, and press the cartridge paper, sticky side down, on to it. Position the decorative paper so that it overlaps at the top edge by about 3in (7.5cm). Smooth flat. Trim level with the cartridge paper, adjusting the top overlap if necessary. Fold along the creases to shape the paper smoothly.

**4** Cut a reinforcing strip of thin card to the same depth as the overlap and as wide as the bag (excluding the side flap) and stick across the top of the cartridge paper. Spread adhesive to the back of the overlap, fold it over the card strip and stick down.

**5** Spread adhesive along the right side of the side flap, and press to the inside edge of the other side of the bag. Align the edges, top and base lines neatly. Press to stick.

**6** To stick down the base, first fold it flat along the crease lines so that the base rests flat against the bag. With a soft pencil, mark the position of the top flap on the other 3 flaps, open out the base

and spread adhesive on the 3 flaps within the pencil marks. Fold the bag flat again and press down the fourth flap in position.

**7** Position the handles to suit the proportions of the bag. Make holes with a hole punch about ¾in (18mm) down from the top edge. Thread cord through the holes and tie knots on the inside.

**8** Make a gift tag to match from a piece of matching giftwrap laminated to card. Or cut out the fan shape from a double thickness of card in a contrasting colour to a plain bag, and decorate with segments of the paper used for the bag. Stick in place. Punch a hole in the tag to

attach decorative thread or narrow ribbon.

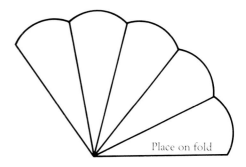

Place on fold

**Trace the fan shape on to a double thickness of card**

# Square box

*A cube-shaped box is always useful, and the pattern can be adapted to make any size of rectangular box. Choose pretty giftwrap to fit the occasion.*

## Materials
Card (thin card is suitable for small boxes, thicker card for larger boxes)
Spray adhesive
Giftwrap
Stick adhesive
25in (62.5cm) of 1⅝in (39mm)-wide ribbon
Thread to match the ribbon
Double-sided sticky tape
2 sequins
Contact glue

## Preparation
1 Decide on the size of box you need and, following the diagram, draw the measurements on to a sheet of card. All angles must be right angles and all the squares must be equal. Cut out the box. Score all the fold lines.

## Working the design
2 Fold along each scored line. Open out.

3 Lay the card flat, creased side facing up and spray with adhesive. Lay out the giftwrap with wrong side facing up and press the card, sticky side down, on to it. Smooth flat and trim the giftwrap level with the card. Fold along the creases to shape the box.

4 Use stick adhesive to stick down the side tab first. Then stick down the tabs at the bottom of the box.

5 To make the ribbon fan, start ½in (12mm) from one end of the ribbon and mark 1in (2.5cm) spaces along one edge

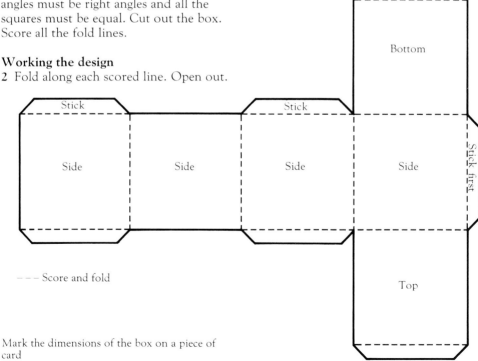

Mark the dimensions of the box on a piece of card

with a soft pencil. Using needle and thread, gather the ribbon through each alternate mark. Pull tight and tie off. Repeat with the alternate marks. Pull tight and tie off.

6 Fold the ends of the ribbon under the fan and stick in place on top of the box with double-sided sticky tape.

7 Stick a sequin to each side of the fan with contact glue.

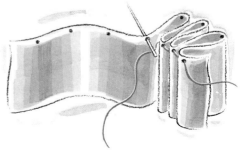

Gather the ribbon through each alternate mark

21

# Long box

*A rectangular box with a lid is always useful. For a special gift, or a romantic occasion, trim the box with a beautiful rose hand-made from crêpe paper.*

**THE BOX**
**Materials**
Thin card
Spray adhesive
Paper to cover (optional)
Ribbon
Double-sided sticky tape

**Preparation**
1 Work out the size of box you need and, following the diagram, draw the measurements for the base of the box on to a sheet of card. 'A' equals the required depth of the box. Cut out the base and score the fold lines.

2 Draw the top of the lid, WXYZ, ⅛in (3mm) larger all round than the base of the box; the 'A' measurement should be smaller than for the base. Cut out the lid and score the fold lines.

**Working the design**
3 Fold both pieces into shape. Open out again.

4 If the box is to be covered, lay each piece of card flat, creased side facing up, and spray with adhesive. Lay out the covering paper, wrong side facing up, and press the base and lid, sticky side down, on to it. Smooth flat, getting rid of air bubbles. Trim the covering paper level with the card edges. Fold along the creases to shape the box.

5 Stick down the end tabs inside the base and lid.

6 Stick pieces of ribbon across the lid of the box with double-sided tape and fix the ends to the inside of the lid.

**THE ROSE**
**Materials**
White crêpe paper
Red water-based paint
Stem wire
Florists' wire
Green crêpe paper
Latex adhesive
2 clear beads with flat backs
Ribbon for bow

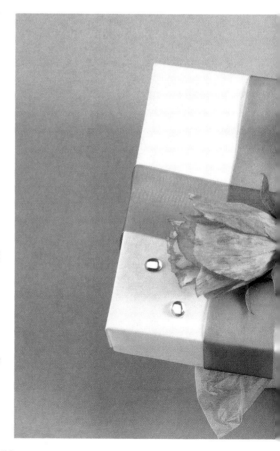

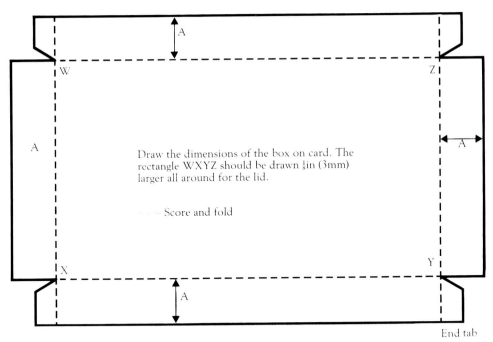

Draw the dimensions of the box on card. The rectangle WXYZ should be drawn ¼in (3mm) larger all around for the lid.

––– Score and fold

W

Z

X

Y

A

A

A

A

End tab

## Preparation

**1** Cut a strip of crêpe paper 2½in (6.5cm) wide from the roll. Unroll the strip and cut a piece from it about 24in (60cm) long. Fold this piece up again so that it measures approximately 1¼in (3cm) across. Cut the petal shape at one end through all layers. Unfold the strip and roll it loosely again.

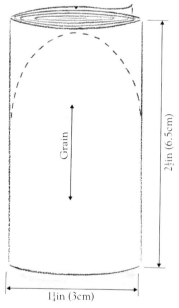

Grain

2½in (6.5cm)

1¼in (3cm)

Cut the petal pattern on 1 edge of a roll of white crêpe paper

**2** Mix some red paint in a shallow dish and, protecting your hands with rubber gloves and the work top with newspaper, dip the petal end of the roll into the paint. Allow it to absorb a little, then squeeze it so that the paint is drawn along the grain of the paper. Allow it to dry in a very low oven. When the crêpe has partially dried, unravel the roll and fold it loosely to allow it to dry thoroughly.

## Working the design

**3** Shape each petal by stretching it widthways with your thumbs. Choose the end of the strip that has the best colouring for the outer petals, and curl the tops of these by rolling them one at a time around a knitting needle.

**4** Use pliers to bend the top of a piece of stem wire into a hook. Wind the petals around the hooked end of the wire, fairly tightly at first, then gathering the base of the petals in your fingers. When you have a satisfactory rose shape, wind florists' wire several times around the base of the petals to secure them.

**5** For the sepals, cut a 2½in (6.5cm) square of green crêpe paper. Fold into 6 with the grain running along the length. Cut into points. Stretch each sepal at the base and curl the tops with a knitting needle. Secure the sepals around the bottom of the rose with latex adhesive.

**6** For the stem, cut a ½in (12mm)-wide strip of green crêpe paper from one edge of the roll. Stick one end to the base of the rose, wind it around the base and down the wire stem, stretching it as you go, and stick down the other end.

**7** Cut a leaf from a double thickness of green crêpe paper. Lay a piece of stem wire down the centre of one leaf, put dots of latex adhesive on each side of the wire and around the edge of the leaf and stick the other leaf-shaped piece on top. Mark veins with the end of a knitting needle and stretch the sides so that it takes the form of a leaf. Bind the stem of the leaf on to the rose stem with a strip of green crêpe paper.

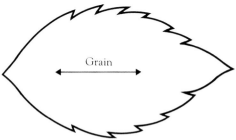

Grain

Cut out each leaf from a double piece of crêpe paper

**8** Stick the finished rose on to the box with latex adhesive. Make a ribbon bow and stick in place. Stick beads on to the box to represent water droplets.

# Fabric wrap

*Gift wrap does not need to be paper and card – the Japanese have been using fabric for centuries. The fabric should be strong but easy to tie into a knot.*

## Materials
Squares of fabric
Ribbon
Double-sided sticky tape

## Preparation
1 As a rough guide for the size of fabric to use, measure the height, width and depth of the gift. Add the 3 measurements together and add on about half as much again to get the length of one side of the fabric. Gifts are wrapped on the diagonal to the fabric, that is, with the sides of the gift facing the corners of the fabric, so that the bias of the fabric can be stretched into shape by pulling at the corners.

## Working the design

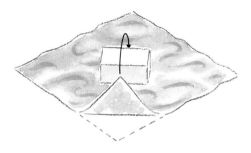

Fold the bottom corner over the gift

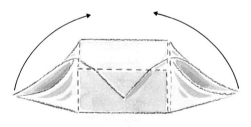

Take the 2 side corners over the gift

2 For a knotted gift wrap: lay out the fabric with the wrong side facing up, and place the gift in the centre. Fold the bottom corner over the gift. Bring the opposite corner over the gift. Take the 2 side corners and bring them together

over the gift, tying a neat knot. Finish with a piece of ribbon wrapped around the gift under the knot, secured with double-sided sticky tape on the bottom.

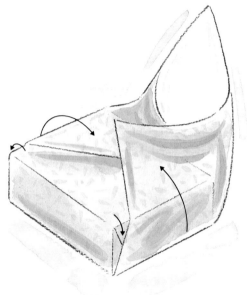

Tuck in the sides neatly and overlap them on top

3 For a tall gift: lay out the fabric with the wrong side facing up, and place the gift diagonally in the centre. Bring all 4 corners to the top, allowing the sides to fall inwards rather than out. Take a piece of narrow ribbon and wind it three or four times around the fabric just above the gift – you will find it easier if someone holds the 4 corners while you do this. Finish with a simple bow. Spread out the corners, twisting them if necessary so that the right side of the fabric shows.

4 For a flatter gift: lay out the fabric with the wrong side facing up, and place the gift diagonally in the centre. Fold the bottom corner over the gift. Fold in the sides neatly and overlap them on top. Bring the top corner over the top, tucking in the sides neatly, and secure the parcel with a narrow ribbon and a simple bow.

26

### Gift-wrapping fabrics

Use a soft fabric that ties easily – satin lining fabric is inexpensive and has a wonderful sheen. Cut out the square to the required size, turn over the edges and machine stitch them, and press.

Alternatively, you can use ready-made squares of fabric that will be part of the gift: a handkerchief, scarf or table napkin or, for a housewarming gift, you could even use a duster.

# Pyramid plant holder

*A potted plant makes an ideal gift but is very difficult to wrap. This attractive pyramid box is simple to make and will set off a plant to perfection.*

## Materials
Thin card

Pictures of butterflies (cut from a sheet of giftwrap or an old card, or draw your own)

Spray adhesive

Cord and tassel or ribbon to tie

## Preparation
1 Draw an equilateral triangle on the card. The length of each side should be at least twice the height of the plant. Use a protractor to ensure that each angle is 60°. Cut out the triangle.

2 Mark the centre of each side and score lines between these points.

## Working the design
3 Fold along each scored line to form the pyramid.

4 Spray the back of the butterflies and stick in place. Alternatively, draw butterflies with felt-tip pens, or stick on flowers cut from giftwrap. Use a craft knife to cut around the wings of some of the butterflies, taking care not to cut across the body. Score a line along the base of the wings on each side of the body and fold the wings out.

5 Punch a hole in each point about ¾in (18mm) from the tip. Tie the box together through the punched holes with cord or ribbon.

---

### Plant holder for a tall plant
For a tall, narrow plant, draw an equilateral triangle slightly larger than the base of the pot in the centre of a piece of coloured card, or card with giftwrap laminated to it. Score along the sides of the triangle. Next, measure the height of the pot and plant. Mark this measurement out from each side of the triangle. Draw lines from the corners of the triangle to the marks, and cut out. Punch a hole in each point about ¾in (18mm) from the tip. Fold up the sides and tie the box together through the punched holes with cord or ribbon. To save wasting card, the sides can be drawn and cut out separately from the base and stuck to the base with sticky tape on the inside.

---

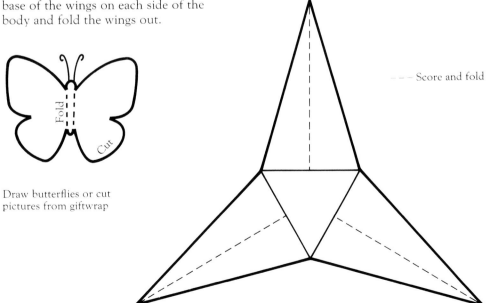

Draw butterflies or cut pictures from giftwrap

– – – Score and fold

Draw lines from the corners to the centre marks

# Elephant box

*Make this box for a child's gift and it will be as popular as the present it conceals. The head and ears are stuck on with adhesive pads to give the 3D effect.*

## ELEPHANT FEATURES
### Materials
Squared paper
Grey card
Square grey box
Black felt-tip pen
Self-adhesive pads
Cord and tassel for the tail
Latex adhesive

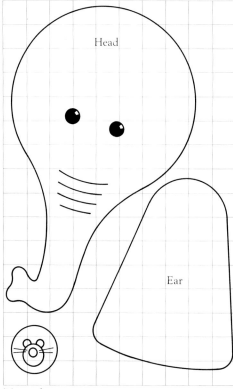

Mouse features

Enlarge on to squared paper and use as templates

### Preparation
1 Enlarge the head and ear pattern on squared paper so that the measurement from the top of the head to the bottom of the trunk is slightly greater than the height of the box, and cut out. Cut out the head and 2 ears from grey card.

### Working the design
2 Draw a line approximately 1in (2.5cm) long in the centre of each side of the box to represent the divisions between the legs. Draw semi-circles on the front of the box for toes. Draw the eyes and trunk wrinkles on the head.

3 Use self-adhesive pads to stick the ears to the front of the box. They should protrude above the top of the box and at each side. Use double-thickness self-adhesive pads to stick on the head, so that it is slightly in front of the ears.

4 Stick a short piece of cord with a tassel to the back of the box with latex adhesive for the tail.

## MOUSE GIFT TAG
### Materials
5 × 3in (12.5 × 7.5cm) of white card
Pink card or paper
Stick adhesive
Black felt-tip pen
Scrap of pink synthetic ribbon

### Preparation
1 Score and fold the card in half.

2 Use a pair of compasses to draw the following diameter circles in pink card or paper and cut them out:
1 × 1⅜in (3.5cm) for the body

1 × 1in (2.5cm) for the head
2 × ⅝in (15mm) for the ears
1 × ½in (12mm) for the snout

## Working the design

**3** Stick the body circle to the bottom of the gift tag. Stick on the ears slightly above the body circle. Stick on the head so that it overlaps the ears and the body. Stick on the snout.

**4** Draw on the features with a black felt-tip pen.

**5** For the mouse's tail, cut a narrow strip of ribbon so that it tapers to a point at one end. Curl the ribbon by gripping it and pulling it gently along its length between your thumb and the blade of a pair of scissors. Stick it in place on the mouse.

# Pillow boxes

*Folded to shape from one piece of card, these attractive boxes are quick and simple to make. They will transform even the smallest gift into a surprise package.*

**Materials**
Thin card
Spray adhesive
Giftwrap (optional)
Stick adhesive
Ribbon

**Preparation**
1 Following the diagram, draw measurements for the size of box you require on a sheet of card. Use a plate as a template to draw the curves. Use a coin to draw the fingertip cut-outs. Cut out the box. Score the fold lines, again using the plate for the curves.

**Working the design**
2 Fold the box into shape. Open it out again.

3 If the box is to be covered, lay it flat, creased side facing up, and spray with

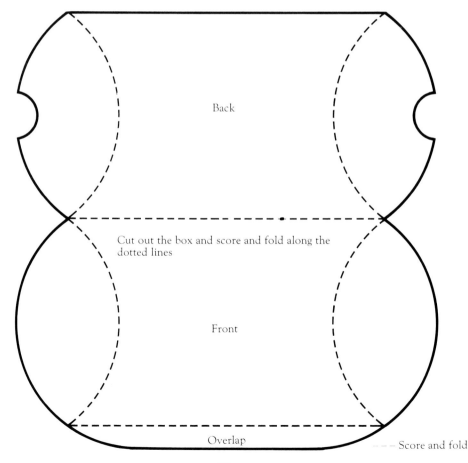

Back

Cut out the box and score and fold along the dotted lines

Front

Overlap

– – – Score and fold

adhesive. Lay out the covering paper, wrong side facing up, and press the card, sticky side down, on to it. Smooth flat. Trim covering level with the card edges. Fold along the creases to shape the box.

**4** Stick the overlap to the inside of the opposite edge. The end flaps do not need to be stuck – they should stay in place when folded. The flaps with the fingertip cut-outs should be folded in first.

**5** Decorate the box with a ribbon rosette or a bow.

### Ribbon rosettes

Use synthetic ribbon that sticks to itself when moistened. Cut 4 pieces 6in (15cm) long. Fold each piece in half to mark the centre. Moisten the centre of each piece and stick them together to make an 8-pointed star. Moisten each end and fold it into the centre to form the first layer of the rosette. Make a second layer in the same way using 5in (12.5cm) pieces of ribbon. Stick this to the first star so that the loops are staggered. Repeat with more layers if wished. Finish the rosette with a single loop made from a short length of ribbon.

# Oval box

*This pretty little box will enhance any gift, and is attractive enough to keep as a useful container. You can make it round or oval and any size you wish.*

**Materials**
Squared paper
Thick card for base and lid
Spray adhesive
Thin card for the sides
Contact glue
Silver paper
Giftwrap
Ribbon
Double-sided sticky tape

**Preparation**
1 Decide on the size of the box, enlarge the oval pattern to the required size on to squared paper, and cut out. Cut out 2 ovals in thick card. Stick the 2 pieces together with spray adhesive.

2 Measure round the circumference of the oval with a tape measure and add ½in (12mm). Cut out a strip of thin card to this length; the width should equal the required depth of the box.

**Working the design**
3 Spread contact glue around the edge of the oval and place it flat on a work surface. Stick one edge of the card strip around the edge of the oval, ensuring that the sides are vertical all the way round. Stick down the overlap.

4 Place the base of the box down on the wrong side of a piece of silver paper and draw round it. Cut out the shape allowing ½in (12mm) extra all around. Cut notches into this margin up to the drawn line. Spray the back with adhesive and lay it flat, sticky side facing up. Press the base of the box on to it, making sure there are no air bubbles, smooth flat, and stick the tabs up around the sides.

5 Cut a strip of giftwrap ½in (12mm) longer than the circumference of the box and ½in (12mm) wider than the depth of the box. Spray the back with adhesive and stick to the sides of the box, lining up the bottom edge just above the bottom of the box. Snip the overlap in several places, fold it over the top and stick to the inside of the box.

6 For the lid, place the base on a double thickness of thick card, draw round it and cut out. Stick the 2 pieces of card together. Cut a strip of thin card for the sides of the lid and stick it to the top piece as for the base.

7 Cut a strip of silver paper 1in (2.5cm) wider than the depth of the lid. Draw lines ½in (12mm) in from each long edge. Cut notches along both long edges up to the drawn lines. Spray the back with adhesive and the strip to the sides of the lid. Fold and stick one notched edge to the top of the lid and the other to the inside of the lid.

8 Place the lid down on the wrong side of a piece of giftwrap, draw round it, and cut it out about ⅛in (3mm) smaller all around. Spray the back of the giftwrap and stick it to the top of the lid. Cut a strip of giftwrap ¼in (6mm) narrower than the depth of the lid. Stick this around the sides.

9 Make a bow to decorate the top and stick it in place with a piece of double-sided sticky tape.

# Cylinder box

*This box was made from a cardboard packing tube. It was covered with tissue paper decorated using a rubber stamp, but it could be covered with pretty giftwrap.*

**Materials**
**For the box:**
Cardboard tube
White paper
Spray adhesive
Thick white card for each end
Thin white card for the lid
Contact glue

Tissue paper (or giftwrap)
Braid

**For rubber stamping:**
Rubber stamp
Ink pad
Gold embossing powder
Heat source (such as a toaster or an iron)

## Preparation

1 Cut the tube to the length required. If the tube is made of very thick cardboard, use a hacksaw to cut it. Sand the cut end flat with sandpaper. To prevent the cardboard showing through tissue paper, cover the outside of the tube with a piece of white paper using spray adhesive.

2 Place the tube upright on a piece of white card and draw around it for the base. Cut it out. Cut out 2 circles of thick card for the top of the lid and stick them together.

3 Cut a strip of thin card, long enough to go round the lid circle with a ½in (12mm) overlap; the width should equal the required depth of the lid. Spread contact glue around the edge of the lid circle and place it flat on a work surface. Apply the edge of the card strip to the edge of the lid circle, keeping the sides vertical.

4 Cut out enough tissue paper to cover the box. You will need: one piece to wrap around the tube with overlaps for the back and each end; one piece to wrap around the lid rim, also with overlaps; and 2 pieces the size of the base circle with a ½in (12mm) overlap all round.

## Working the design

5 Working on one small area at a time, stamp the rubber stamp on the tissue sheets, turning the stamp at different angles. For the tissue that will be wrapped around the sides of the lid, stamp the images in a row. Stamp 1 image in the centre for the lid. As you stamp each image, pour embossing powder on to it, ensuring that the whole image is covered. Shake off the excess powder on to a folded sheet of clean paper and return to the container. When you have covered 3 or 4 images, hold the tissue paper, image upwards, over the heat source, taking care not to let it touch it, to melt the powder.

6 Cover the tube first. Spray adhesive on the back of the appropriate piece of

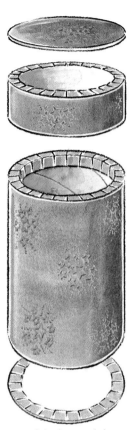

Cover each part of the box and then assemble it

tissue and stick it around the tube, overlapping it at the back. Cut slits into the overlap at each end and fold and stick to the inside of the tube. Next spray the back of the tissue circle for the bottom of the tube. Stick the card circle in the centre, cut notches in the overlap and fold and stick to the back. Spread contact glue around the bottom edge of the tube and stick on to the back of the covered circle to form the bottom of the box.

7 Cover the sides of the lid with the strip of tissue, cutting, folding and sticking the overlapping pieces to the inside and top of the lid. Cut another card circle to fit the top of the lid and cover this with the last piece of tissue. Stick the covered card circle on to the top of the lid.

8 Decorate the top and bottom edges of the lid with narrow braid.

# TWO

# Greetings for all occasions

# Zig-zag penguins

Anyone, especially a youngster, would be delighted to receive these perky penguins on their birthday. They fold up concertina fashion to fit into an envelope.

## Materials
Paper for patterns
$6\frac{1}{2} \times 11\frac{1}{4}$in (16.5 × 28.5cm) piece of thin
  black card
White paper
Orange paper or card
Black paper
Spray adhesive

## Preparation
1 Trace and make paper patterns for
each of the penguins.

2 Measure and score lines across the
black card $2\frac{3}{8}$in (6cm), 5in (12.5cm), and
8in (20cm) from one end. Fold into a zig-
zag. Open it out again.

## Working the design
3 Draw around each of the penguins on
the appropriately sized section of black
card, keeping all of the penguins level
with the bottom edge. Cut out the card.

4 Cut out the chests in white paper, the
beaks and feet in orange paper and the
eyes in white and black paper. Spray a
spare piece of white paper lightly with
adhesive and lay the cut-out pieces on
this (this will prevent the small pieces
moving when they are sprayed). Spray
the backs with adhesive, ease them off the
backing paper with a craft knife and stick
in place on the penguins. Draw a line
along the beak in black pen.

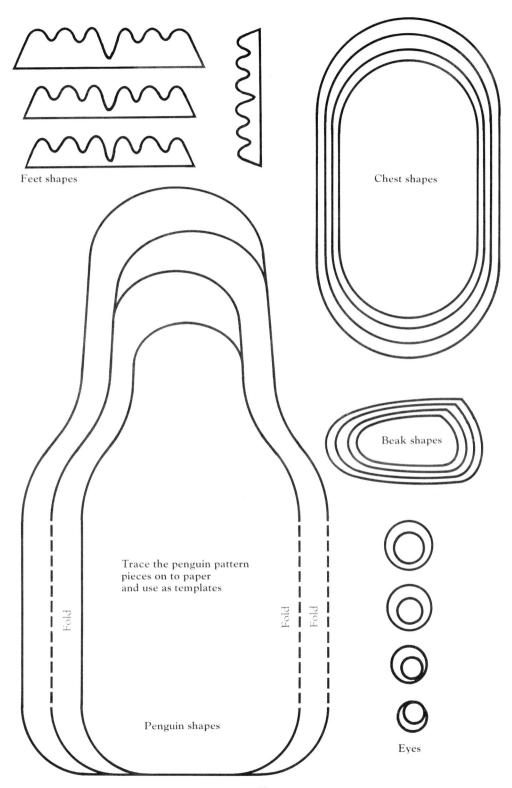

Feet shapes

Chest shapes

Beak shapes

Trace the penguin pattern
pieces on to paper
and use as templates

Fold

Fold

Fold

Penguin shapes

Eyes

43

# Silver bells

*These bells are cut out on both sides and twisted so that they stand out, although they lie flat for the post. Any simple shape or number can be cut in the same way.*

## Materials
7 × 8in (18 × 20cm) piece of light grey card
White and grey paper
Spray adhesive
Card for template
Silver paper
Cord and tassel

## Preparation
1 Mark the centre on the 7in (18cm) sides of the grey card. Score a line between these points and fold the card in half.

2 Cut a piece of white paper $2\frac{3}{4} \times 7\frac{1}{4}$in (7 × 18.5cm). Spray the back with adhesive and stick it to a larger piece of grey paper. Cut out the grey paper leaving a margin of about $\frac{1}{8}$in (3mm). Spray the back and stick it to the front of the card.

3 Trace the bell on to spare card and cut out to make a template.

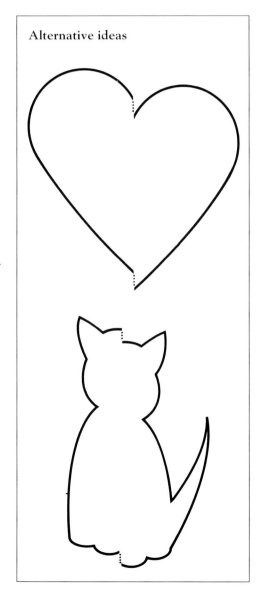

Alternative ideas

Trace the bell on to card and cut out

Cut solid lines, score and fold along dotted lines

44

## Working the design

**4** Use the template to cut out 3 bells in silver paper. Spray the backs and stick them to the card, positioning them carefully.

**5** Open the card and lay it flat, right side facing up, on a protected work surface. Carefully cut around both sides of each

bell with a sharp craft knife. Score the fold lines at the top and bottom of each bell. You should now be able to twist each bell so that it stands out.

**6** Punch a hole across the fold of the card approximately $\frac{1}{2}$in (12mm) from the top. Thread a cord and tassel through the hole.

# Flower collage

*Flowers are always acceptable for birthdays, Mother's Day, Get Well or Thanks. These are made using tissue paper, which is layered and overlapped to look like petals.*

**Materials**
Thin white card
Coloured tissue paper for the flowers and leaves
Spray adhesive
Scrap of brown paper
Green felt-tip pen

**Preparation**
1 Cut a piece of white card 6½ × 10in (16.5 × 25cm) (the size can be adjusted according to the size of envelope available). Mark the centre of the long sides, score a line between these points and fold in half. Use a plate as a template to draw a curve in pencil around the top right-hand corner on the front of the card.

2 Trace and make templates for the petals, leaves and pot.

3 Laminate 2 layers of green tissue together with spray adhesive, using dark green tissue for the cyclamen or bright green for the geranium.

**Working the design**
4 For each card, cut out 1 pot in brown paper, 7 or 8 leaves in double thickness green tissue and several petals in red or pink tissue. Up to 8 layers of tissue can be cut out at once – fold the tissue and draw around the template on to the top layer.

5 Spray the back of the pot with adhesive and stick it to the card. For the leaves and petals you will find it easier to first lightly spray a sheet of white paper with adhesive so that it becomes slightly tacky. Lay the leaves and petals on this sheet before spraying them. They can be

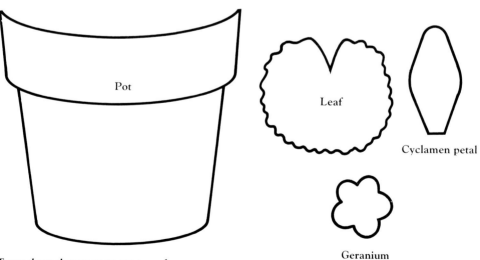

Pot

Leaf

Cyclamen petal

Geranium

Trace these shapes on to paper and use as templates

46

eased off the paper with the edge of a craft knife and positioned on the card. Arrange the cyclamen petals in fours, with the petals in each group overlapping each other. Arrange the geranium petals in groups of 5 or 6, overlapping the petals in each group.

6 Open the card. Use a sharp craft knife to cut around the drawn curve on the corner and to cut away areas between some of the flowers and around their outer edges.

7 Draw in some stems with a green pen.

47

# Quilled music cards

*This idea can be adapted for any occasion. Copy a line from a popular song or, for Christmas, use the first line of a carol and decorate with quilled bells.*

**Materials**
Coloured paper or paper quilling strips
Card blank
Clear-drying glue
Quilling tool (this can be made by embedding the point of a darning needle in an eraser and filing off the end of the eye to create a slit)

**Preparation**
1 To make your own quilling strips, determine the direction of the grain on the coloured paper. This can be done by tearing it, as it will tear more easily with the grain. Use a sharp craft knife and metal rule to cut strips along the grain $\frac{1}{8}$in (3mm) wide. Take great care to cut strips that are even in width along their whole length.

2 Choose the music and determine the length of the lines that you can fit across the card. Use a black pen to draw the lines across the card $\frac{1}{10}$in (2mm) apart.

## Working the design

3 To make a coil, place one end of a paper strip into the slit of the quilling tool. Hold it in place with one hand while gently turning the tool with the other hand until all the paper has been used up. Slip the coil from the tool. If a loose coil is required, allow it to spring open to the required size before shaping it. For a tight coil, put a spot of glue on the end of the strip to secure it.

4 To make the notes: For crotchets, use a 3½in (9cm) strip. Make a tight coil with a ½in (12mm) tail. For semibreves, use a 1in (2.5cm) strip. For double-crotchets, use a 7½in (19cm) strip. Make a tight coil on each end and allow 1½in (4cm) in the centre to fold into shape. The treble clefs are made in 2 pieces. For the top use a 3½in (9cm) strip wound into a loose coil at one end, with the other end folded loosely back on itself and stuck in place. The tail is made from a 1½in (4cm) strip wound into a loose coil at one end. The central upright of the treble clef is drawn in ink, as are the sharps, etc.

5 To make the decorative shapes: These are made with loose coils, which are then pinched into shape.

6 Position the coils on the card and stick in place.

Treble clefs are made in 2 parts

Heart: fold strip in half, then roll each end towards the inside

Petal: loose scroll pinched at one end

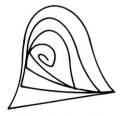

Leaf: loose scroll pinched at both ends

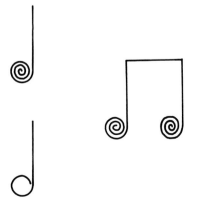

Bell: loose scroll, pinched on both sides at the bottom

# Victorian paper lace

*Pictures from old cards are used for these Victorian-looking cards. The lace effect on the surround is created by piercing paper with two different-sized needles.*

## Materials

Tapestry needle and darning needle
Large eraser
Old greetings cards
Tracing paper
White or coloured cartridge paper
Sticky tape
Manicure scissors with curved blades
Spray adhesive
Paper to contrast with chosen pictures

## Preparation

**1** Make a handle for the needles by embedding each one in opposite ends of the eraser.

**2** Cut suitable pictures from old cards in an oval shape 3½in (8.5cm) high and 2¾in (7cm) wide.

**3** Trace the half-border design on to folded tracing paper, then trace the other half to the complete design.

**4** Try out the lace effect on a spare piece of paper. Holes pierced from the wrong side of the paper have greater definition, while holes pierced from the right side are smooth and less obtrusive. Space the holes equally, and not too close together, otherwise the paper may tear.

## Working the design

**5** Lay the tracing on a sheet of cartridge paper and secure with sticky tape along one edge. Lay both on top of a padded surface such as a folded blanket. Prick out the inner and outer lines with the larger needle. The paper can be turned over for the scrolls and pierced through from the back, making sure that the holes already pierced are lined up with the tracing. Pierce the scrolls with the smaller needle.

**6** Carefully cut around the border with curved scissors.

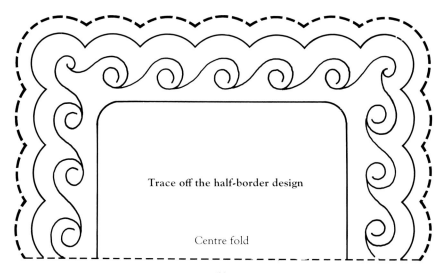

Trace off the half-border design

Centre fold

7 Spray the back of the picture and stick it to the contrasting coloured paper. Cut out the paper approximately ⅛in (3mm) larger all around than the picture. Spray the back with adhesive and stick it to the centre of the paper lace.

8 Make a support for the back of the card with a 1½ × 5in (4 × 12.5cm) strip of cartridge paper. Fold over 1in (2.5cm) at one end and stick this tab to the back of the card so that the other end is level with the bottom of the card.

# Christmas tree

*Whoever receives this card will probably use it as a Christmas decoration. It folds flat for the post and one side can be lined with plain paper for your message.*

**Materials**
Giftwrap in 2 contrasting colours
12 × 9in (30 × 23cm) piece of coloured card
Spray adhesive
Gold thread

**Preparation**
1 Enlarge the tree pattern to a height of 20cm (8 in) cut out 2 trees in each colour giftwrap. If you prefer, 1 side of the tree can be lined with plain paper, so substitute 1 of the giftwrap tree shapes

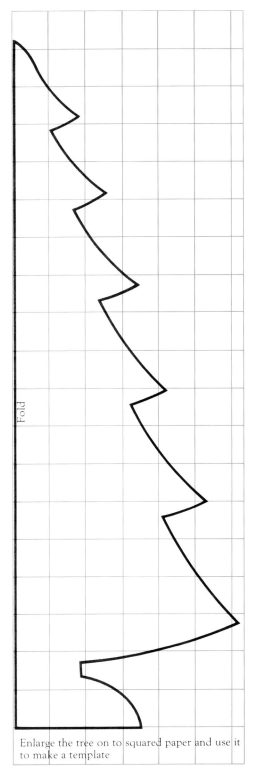

Enlarge the tree on to squared paper and use it to make a template

with plain paper. Fold each piece in half.

**2** Cut a 6 × 9in (15 × 23cm) piece of coloured card. Mark the centre of the 6in (15cm) sides and score a line between the points. Fold the card in half.

### Working the design
**3** Spray the back of one of the giftwrap trees with adhesive. Open the folded card and lay it flat with the inside surface facing up. Lay the giftwrap tree, sticky side down on to the card, ensuring that the centre folds are lined up. Cut around the edge of the card approximately $\frac{1}{8}$in (3mm) from the edge of the giftwrap. Stick a contrasting giftwrap tree to the back.

**4** Using the card you have just cut out as a template, cut out a second card tree. Fold it in half. Stick a giftwrap tree to one side and the last giftwrap tree, or the plain paper tree, to the other side.

**5** Hold the cards with the 2 matching pieces of giftwrap facing each other and use a needle and gold thread to sew both cards together with a few large stitches in the fold line.

Sew both card trees together with a few large stitches

# Easter bunny

*The Easter bunny is mounted on a spring so that it wobbles. The same technique could be used for any card using a figure or animal cut from an old card.*

**Materials**
8 × 10in (20 × 25cm) piece of cream card
White card
White wool for the tail
10in (25cm) of florists' binding wire
Green tissue paper
Spray adhesive
Cream paper
Pink paper
Self-adhesive pads
Latex adhesive
Clear sticky tape
Yellow paper for flowers

**Preparation**
1  Score and fold the cream card in half.

2  Trace the bunny outline on to white card. Cut out a complete bunny and an extra head.

3  Make a tiny white pompom for the tail.

4  To make the spring, wind the wire tightly around a pencil several times so that the coil is about ¾in (18mm) long.

Trace the bunny outline on to card

## Working the design

**5** Tear the tissue paper into strips and spray the back with adhesive. Stick the tissue strips in overlapping layers on to the cream paper, leaving an area for the sky. Trim the edges with a craft knife so that the paper measures $6\frac{3}{4} \times 3\frac{3}{4}$in ($17 \times 9.5$cm). Spray the back with adhesive and stick it in the centre of the pink paper. Trim the pink paper so that there is a $\frac{1}{4}$in (6mm) margin. Spray the back with adhesive and stick it in the centre of the card front.

**6** Trace the inner ears and cut out in pink paper. Stick to the head and draw on the features. Stick the head to the complete bunny with self-adhesive pads. Stick the pompom to the tail with latex adhesive.

**7** Use small pieces of sticky tape to attach one end of the spring to the back of the bunny and the other end to the card.

**8** Cut out a few flower heads in yellow paper and stick in place.

# New home

*Everyone appreciates a card when they move, especially if it is hand-made. The tiny house and beehive on these cards are made with oven-baked modelling clay.*

## Materials

Brown oven-baked modelling clay for the beehive

Red and pink oven-baked modelling clay for the house

6 × 8in (15 × 20cm) piece of pastel-coloured card

3in (7.5cm) square of paper to tone with the card

Spray adhesive

Contact adhesive

Red paper for the hearts or orange paper for the bees

⅛in (3mm) strips of coloured paper

## Preparation

1 For the beehive, roll a long thin strip of brown clay. Cut it into 1in (2.5cm) pieces and press them together on a baking tray. Cut the edges into a beehive shape. Use the end of a plastic drinking straw to cut away the opening. Bake according to the instructions on the packet.

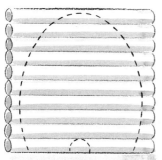

Beehive

2 For the house, roll out a piece of red and a piece of pink clay to about ⅛in (3mm) thick. Cut out the house wall in pink clay and lay it on a baking tray. Cut the roof shape in red clay and press it to

the house wall. Cut away the door and cut a piece of red clay to fit in its place. Use the point of a craft knife to make markings to represent the window, roof shingles, etc. Bake according to the instructions on the packet.

House

## Working the design

3 Score and fold the card in half. Spray the back of the paper square with adhesive and stick to the front of the card so that there is a ½in (12mm) margin at the top and sides.

4 Stick the hive or house in place with contact adhesive.

5 Cut out hearts in red paper or ovals in orange paper for the bees, and stick in place. Draw the bees' wings, stripes and feelers in black pen.

Body for bee

Heart

6 Stick on strips of coloured paper to frame the paper square.

# Cross-stitch card

*You can embroider your own message on this card – simply adjust the length of the banner. It is worked on perforated paper but could be worked on fabric.*

**Materials**
Squared paper
White perforated paper with 14 divisions
 to 1in (2.5cm)
Red, black, blue and flesh-coloured
 stranded embroidery cotton
Parchment card
Clear-drying all-purpose adhesive

**Preparation**
1 Decide on your message and write it
out on squared paper. Adjust the length
of the banner to fit the message and
position the fold between 2 words. Draw

the rest of the design around the banner.
Count the divisions in your finished
drawing and mark the centre.

2 For the banner outline and the aircraft
outline and details use a single strand of
black embroidery cotton. For all other
areas, use 3 strands of embroidery
cotton.

**Working the design**
3 Work the aircraft and the hearts in
cross stitch. Work the aircraft outline
and details in back stitch.

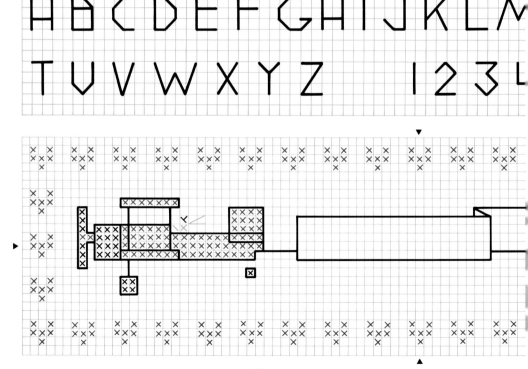

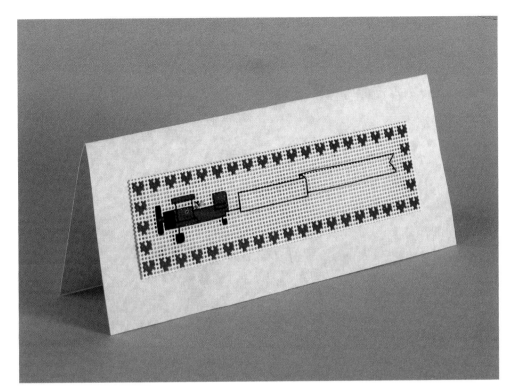

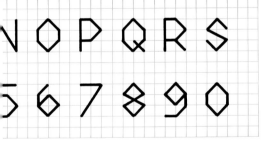

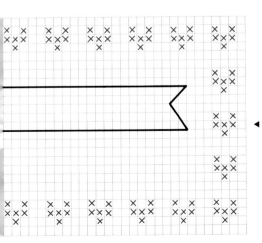

**4** The pilot consists of a combination of small individual stitches: a single cross stitch in blue for the body; a three-quarter cross stitch in black for the helmet, with another three-quarter cross stitch in flesh colour for the face, both worked in the same square; a half cross stitch in blue for the arm; and 2 straight stitches for the pilot's scarf.

**5** Work the banner outline in long straight stitches and the lettering in back stitch.

**6** Cut out the design 1 division from the edge of the hearts.

**7** Cut a piece of parchment card so that when folded in half it is approximately 1½in (4cm) wider and deeper than your finished embroidery. Spread adhesive on the back of the hearts and stick the embroidery in the centre of the card.

Follow the chart to stitch the design

# Felt and stitched card

*This card can be made for many different occasions – Sorry I forgot, Get Well Soon, or just Best Wishes. Only the flowers, tail and eye are embroidered.*

**Materials**
Fusible web
Grey felt
Pink felt

Green, black and red stranded
    embroidery cotton
Card with a round pre-cut window
Contrasting coloured paper
All-purpose glue

Trace the elephant and ear shapes on to the back of the fusible webbing

## Preparation
1 Iron fusible web on to the back of a small piece of grey felt. Trace and transfer the elephant pattern to the paper backing of the fusible web. Cut out the elephant and the ear.

2 Remove the paper backing and iron the elephant on to pink felt. Iron the ear on to the body.

## Working the design
3 Using 2 strands of thread, work the flower stems and tail in straight stitch.

4 Work french knots for the flower heads and the elephant's eye.

## Finishing
5 Cut the pink felt to the size of the card.

6 Cut a circle slightly smaller than that in the card from the contrasting coloured paper. Spread glue thinly on the wrong side and place it, sticky side down, on to the embroidery. Press firmly and leave to dry.

7 Spread glue thinly round the window on the inside of the card and place the paper-framed embroidery in position. Press firmly and leave to dry.

8 Glue the return fold around the embroidery and press firmly.

## Alternative ideas
The same idea can be adapted for other occasions using a combination of felt shapes with a few simple embroidery stitches. For Christmas, cut 2 circles of white felt for a snowman and a square of black for his hat. Embroider french knots for eyes and nose and use straight stitch for the hat brim, scarf and mouth. Make a good luck cat from circles and triangles of black felt and embroider the whiskers in straight stitch.

# Pop-up heart

*Perfect for Valentine's Day, this pop-up card is decorated with a rubber stamp and embossed in gold, but you could just stick on hearts cut from pretty paper or doyleys.*

## Materials
### For the card:
9 × 12in (23 × 30cm) of cartridge-weight paper in red or crimson
Contrasting colour paper
Spray adhesive

### For rubber stamping:
Heart-shaped rubber stamp
Stamp pad
Gold embossing powder
Heat source (such as a toaster or an iron)
Felt or fibre-tip pens
Embossing pen

## Preparation
**1** Score a line 4½in (11.5cm) from one of the shorter sides of the red paper and fold. The smaller section will form the outside of the card. Open out and score a line down the centre of the paper at right angles to the first. Fold and unfold. You should now be able to fold the paper into a card shape with the fold at the bottom.

**2** Open out again and draw the heart in the centre of the inside of the card. The top of the heart should be on the top edge of the paper and the diagonal lines on the heart should be level with the top of the outside of the card. Cut away the paper around the top half of the heart. It should now protrude from the top.

Fold the paper into a card shape

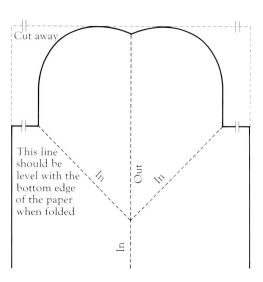

Cut away

This line should be level with the bottom edge of the paper when folded

In

Out

In

In

Position the heart on the paper

## Working the design
**3** To make the heart fold inside the card, score the diagonal lines. Now carefully fold the centre line of the heart out, and the diagonals in. Fold and unfold several times so that it works smoothly.

**4** Stamp the heart design on the contrasting colour paper. As each image is stamped, pour embossing powder on to it, ensuring that the whole image is covered. Shake off the excess powder on to a folded sheet of clean paper so that it can be poured back into the container. Hold the paper, image upwards, over the heat source, taking care not to let it touch the heat source, to melt the powder. Colour parts of the design with pens if wished.

**5** Cut out one heart for the pop-up, cutting it out with a gently rippling effect. Fold it in half and spray the back with adhesive. Stick it on to the pop-up heart, carefully lining up the fold lines. Cut another heart for the front of the card and stick in place. Draw a simple design on the bottom corners of the inside of the card with the embossing pen and emboss in gold.

**Hints on rubber stamping**
Push the stamp well down in the stamp pad to achieve an even coverage.

Take care not to twist or move the stamp at all when pressing it on to the paper. Clean rubber stamps with a little diluted washing-up liquid after use and store them rubber side up.

# Origami pigs

*Origami is the Japanese art of paper folding. The traditional pig design is folded from squares of pretty giftwrap to make an attractive greetings card.*

## Materials

Giftwrap
Contrasting colour card
Pink paper for hearts
Spray adhesive

## Preparation

1 Cut 6in (15cm) squares of giftwrap.

## Working the design

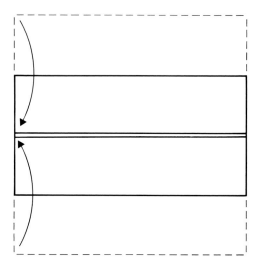

2 For each pig, use a square of paper, wrong side up. (It is advisable to practise the folds first on thin copy paper.) Fold the paper in half from bottom to top to mark the centre. Unfold, then fold the top edge and the bottom edge into the centre.

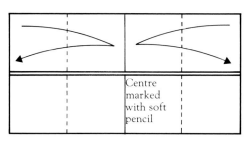

3 Measure across the width and mark the centre line with a soft pencil. Fold each side into the centre. Press flat and unfold.

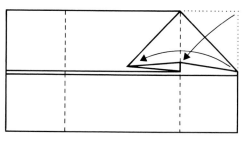

4 Insert your finger between the upper right-hand layers of paper and pull the top layer over towards the centre. Press the paper down neatly into a triangle.

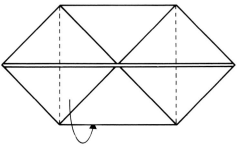

5 Repeat steps 3 and 4 with the other 3 corners. Fold in half taking the bottom half behind.

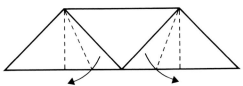

6 To make the legs, fold the inner points over so that the sloping edge meets the fold line.

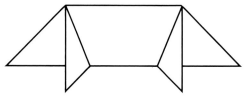

7 The paper should look like this. Turn it over and make the 2 legs on the other side.

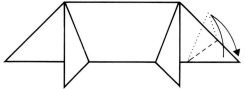

8 For the snout, fold and unfold the right-hand point.

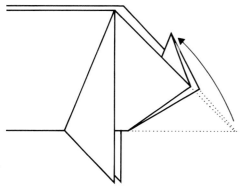

9 Now push the point up inside the model along the fold lines just made and press flat.

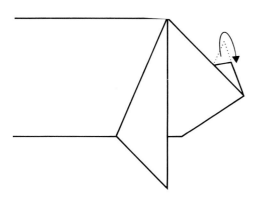

10 Fold over the end of the snout.

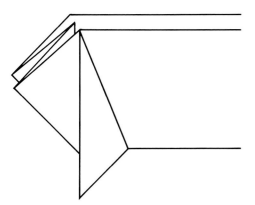

11 For the tail, fold and unfold the left-hand point. Push the point up inside the model along the fold lines just made and press flat.

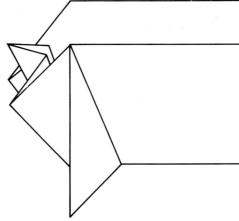

12 Fold this point back on itself in the same way to complete the tail.

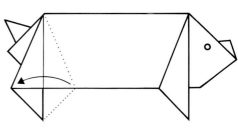

13 Fold back the 2 back legs. Draw in the eye and rub out the pencilled centre line.

**Finishing**
14 Make a long single-fold card. Cut 2 hearts in pink paper. Use spray adhesive to stick pigs and heart to the card.

**Trace 2 hearts on to pink paper**

67

# Rocking card

*Make your Christmas greeting extra special with a rocking card, such as this angel. It is ideal to send to children, who will love setting it in motion.*

**Materials**
Gold card
Flesh-coloured paper
Paper doyley
6in (15cm) piece of gold cord
Gold thread
Silver lurex
Scrap of black paper
Red pen
All-purpose glue
Latex adhesive

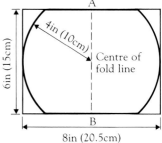

6in (15cm)

4in (10cm)

Centre of
fold line

A

B

8in (20.5cm)

Draw the basic dimensions for the angel on card

**Preparation**
**1** For the base cut a 6 × 8in (15 × 20.5cm) piece of gold card. Score across the card halfway along its length and fold in half. Mark the centre of the folded edge. Open out the card and with a compass set at 4in (10cm), draw an arc at each end of the card. Cut along the line of the arc.

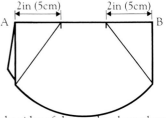

2in (5cm)    2in (5cm)

A                                      B

Draw in the sides of the angel and cut along the line through the double thickness of card

**2** Fold the card back in half. Mark 2in (5cm) in from one side of the fold. Draw a line from this point to the edge of the curve. Cut along this line through the double thickness of card. Repeat on the other side.

**3** Cover the front of the card with part of a doyley, securing it with dots of glue.

**4** Cut 1¼in (3cm)-radius circles of gold card and flesh-coloured paper for the head. Stick the two circles together and stick the head to the front of the folded card.

Position of the head and arms

**5** Trace the wings on to gold card and stick to the back of the figure, the top of the wings level with the fold in the card.

**6** Cut out the arms from flesh-coloured paper and cover the tops with pieces cut from a doyley. Stick in position.

**7** Cut eyes from black paper and stick in place. Mark nose with a red pen.

**8** To make the hair, tie a piece of gold thread around the centre of the gold cord. Unravel the ends of the cord to the centre. Spread latex adhesive over the top and sides of the head and stick the hair in place, bringing some strands forward to form a fringe. Trim the fringe and tie the sides in bunches with silver lurex.

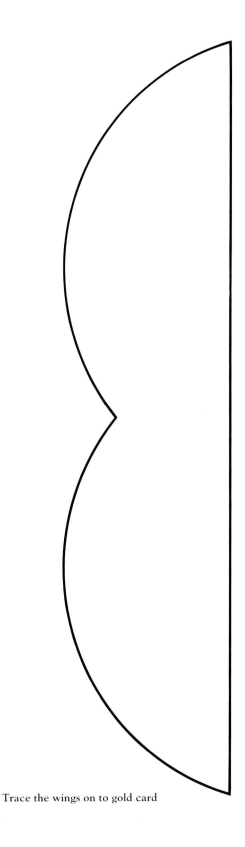

**Trace the wings on to gold card**

# Parchment craft

*This attractive card to celebrate the birth of a new baby was made in parchment craft. The design is traced in ink, then embossed by pressing through from the back.*

## Materials

Masking tape
Parchment paper (heavy draughtsman's
    paper)
Pen
White ink
Small ball-tip embossing tool
Felt pad
Red or blue ink
A needle and a large eraser

## Preparation

1 Use masking tape to stick a piece of
parchment paper over the design,
allowing for the fold of the card and a
margin of approximately $\frac{1}{2}$in (12mm)
around the other 3 edges.

## Working the design

2 Trace the design in white ink.

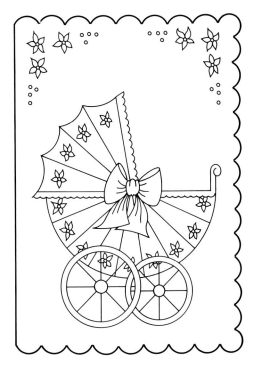

Trace the design through parchment paper

3 Embossing: Lay the parchment paper
ink side down on the felt pad. Emboss all
the lines by gently pressing with the

embossing tool on the back of the design.
This has the effect of raising the lines on
the right side, and as the paper is
stretched it turns white. Emboss each
petal separately with evenly applied
strokes, working the tool from the centre
of the flower to the point of the petal.
Lastly, emboss areas of the bow so
that parts of it stand out, giving a
3-dimensional effect.

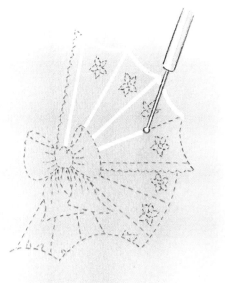

Emboss the lines from the back

4 Painting: Mix a little red or blue ink
with some white in a shallow dish making
a pale pink or blue. Paint the petals,
allowing the outer tips to remain white.
Paint the embossed parts of the bow.
Add a little more red or blue to your
paint mixture to make a deeper colour
and go over the inner parts of the petals,
and parts of the bow.

5 Fold the card in half.

6 Perforating: Insert the eye of the needle
into the eraser to make a perforating
tool. Working around the outer edges of
the scalloped line, pierce holes close
together through both thicknesses. You
should now be able to tear off the outer
edges carefully, leaving an attractive
perforated edge.

# Better Techniques

*This chapter provides useful information about selecting paper and card, and what tools to use, and shows you how to make other things that you will need.*

## PAPER AND CARD

It is important to choose suitable paper and card both for giftwrap and for making greetings cards.

Greetings cards should be made from card which, when folded, will not fall over and which is thick enough that the edges don't curl. However, they should not be too heavy for the post. Use card weighing 134–201 lb/sq in (200–300gsm) – most good craft shops and stationers have the weights marked.

Card for boxes will vary according to the size of box. For a small box, or the sides of a box that needs to be curved, use thin card of about 201 lb/sq in (300gsm). For the base and lid of a curved box, or for larger boxes, use heavier weight card, about 268–368 lb/sq in (400–550gsm).

Experiment with different types of paper and card, as often the paper itself will give you ideas for a card. There are some beautiful shades of recycled card and paper on the market, and a wide range of pastel-coloured watercolour papers with a gently textured surface. Pads of watercolour paper are available with assorted colours, and it is a good idea to buy an A5 pad if you are making several cards. Pastel colours can be enhanced by the use of narrow margins of a brighter, toning colour – stick your design on to a piece of coloured copy paper and cut it out leaving an ⅛in (3mm) margin. Then stick the copy paper to the front of your card. Or use strips of quilling paper to frame a design.

Card blanks, available in most craft shops, are invaluable in making your own cards and provide a professional finish. Some have embossed edges, with plain centres where you stick your design. Window cards are available in all shapes, sizes and colours. They consist of a card with 3 sections, and a window cut from the centre section. You stick your design behind the window, fold the right-hand section behind the window and stick it down to make a neat card.

Tissue papers are available in a wide colour range, and different colour effects can be obtained by overlapping it in layers. Tissue paper is also useful for covering boxes, and a lovely effect can be obtained by using rubber stamps and embossing powders on the paper before covering the box. Many other papers can be used in this way, including delicate papers such as Mulberry paper or even plain brown paper.

Crêpe paper, too, comes in a wide colour range and is extremely versatile. Experiment with different colours – yellow dipped in red paint, squeezed and dried, makes beautiful rose petals.

The choice of giftwrap paper is enormous. Use good-quality giftwrap that folds and creases well without cracking. Foil papers are useful for added sparkle, but are difficult to stick over large areas and tend to bubble when laminated to card. They are best in small amounts for decorating motifs, background margins and covering the edges of small boxes.

## TOOLS AND EQUIPMENT

Most equipment required for making cards and giftwrap is readily available, and you will probably already have most things. However, there are a few specialist pieces of equipment that you will find helpful.

The work surface is important. This should be at a good working height, flat and stable. You will need to protect the work surface when using craft knives, to prevent it from being scratched. A sheet of thick card or board provides suitable protection, but as it will quickly become pitted from successive knife cuts, it may be worth buying a special cutting mat. This has a surface that 'heals itself' after every cut and thus lasts a long time and remains smooth.

The work surface should also be protected with newspaper when you are using paints and sprays. You will find a pair of rubber gloves useful to protect your hands when using paints.

### Cutting tools

You will need a good-quality craft knife for cutting card and paper. A scalpel with straight blades is suitable for most tasks. If the blades are changed frequently, this can be used for cutting even thick card, although you may have to run the knife along the cutting line two or three times. Take care when using knives. You should always cut straight lines by lining up the knife against a firm straight edge such as a metal rule.

You will need a few pairs of sharp scissors. A pair of fairly small, easy-to-handle scissors with straight-pointed blades is suitable for most cutting jobs. For small intricate shapes and curving edges, a pair of manicure scissors with curved blades is more useful. A pair of tweezers is useful for handling small cut-out shapes.

A pair of compasses that has provision for a cutting needle is useful. The needle is inserted in the arm of the compass that normally holds the lead, and is invaluable for cutting circles and large curves so that they are straight and even.

### Cutting paper and card

To cut card, lay it flat on a protected surface. Draw the pattern outline directly on to the card. Use a set square and ruler to check right angles and parallel lines. Line up a straight metal edge against the line to be cut. Press the craft knife against the metal edge, and firmly draw the knife towards you, keeping an even pressure on the straight edge to keep it still. Score the cutting line gently to mark it (and if only marking fold lines), then, still with the straight edge in position, cut along the line again, pressing harder. For thick card, you may have to cut along the line a third time to cut right through.

A plate can be used as a template for curved lines. The plate should be placed upside down on the surface, and the blade of the knife lined up against the edge of the plate and drawn towards you. For other curves, mark the shape lightly with the knife point, and cut round it making sure your free hand is pressing firmly on the card to keep it still, and that your fingers are not in line with the knife, should it slip.

When cutting small intricate shapes with the curved manicure scissors, keep the curve of the blades away from you so that you can see where you are cutting. Birds and animals, and even some flowers and foliage, are best cut out with feathered edging to give a more realistic effect. To do this, first cut out the section, roughly following the outline of that part of the picture. Then cut the edge to be feathered, cutting out 'V' shapes using straight cuts but cutting at different angles and different lengths, to create a ragged effect.

The edges of cards can be cut with a gently rippling effect to give a softer silhouette. This is done with the curved scissors.

## Drawing equipment

A few items of geometry equipment are also useful. You will need a pair of compasses, a set square and a ruler with small measurement markings. A protractor is useful for drawing accurate angles. Other tools include a selection of HB and soft pencils, felt-tip pens, and a good-quality eraser.

---

## USING GEOMETRY EQUIPMENT
### Protractor

This is a half-circle of plastic with degrees marked along the curved edge from 0° to 180°. To measure an angle, turn the paper or card so that the line from which you wish to draw the angle is horizontal. Place the protractor so that the centre of the 0°–180° line is on the point from which you wish to draw the angle, and the 0°–180° line is in line with the horizontal line on your drawing. Find the desired degree on the edge of the protractor and put a small pencilled mark by it. Remove the protractor and, with a ruler, draw a line from the pencilled mark to the point from which you have measured the angle.

### Pair of compasses

These have a steel point at the end of one arm, and either a lead at the end of the other arm, or a hole through which a pencil can be inserted and screwed in place. Measure the radius of the desired circle on a ruler using the two arms. Fix the point into the paper lightly and swing the pencil round in a complete circle.

---

## Adhesives and tapes

Choose the right adhesive tape for the job. Double-sided sticky tape is useful for sticking two surfaces together where you do not want any tape to show, for example sticking ribbon to a parcel, or sticking the overlap on a parcel. Ordinary transparent sticky tape is useful where it is not important if the tape shows, although it is now available in a virtually invisible version. Masking tape peels off easily, so is useful for temporarily sticking paper or card to the work surface so that it does not move. Self-adhesive pads are sticky on both sides and a few millimetres thick. They are used for raising an image slightly from the surface.

PVA is a multi-purpose, easy-to-use adhesive, which dries transparent. Clear, quick-drying and non-trailing craft glue is a good multi-purpose adhesive for card and paper. Stick adhesive is required in some projects. This type of adhesive comes in a roll-up tube and is easy to control. Fast-bonding glues are used to stick different types of material together, although extreme caution should be used with these or you may end up becoming very attached to your work! Never allow children to use these glues. Another useful glue is latex adhesive. This can also be used as a contact adhesive and for bonding different types of material together. Apply sparingly and evenly to both surfaces. Allow it to become touch dry then bring both surfaces together.

## Spray adhesive

This is used to laminate large or very small areas of paper together without stretching or dampening the paper. It is the ideal adhesive to stick giftwrap to boxes, or it can be used to strengthen thin paper by laminating it to thicker paper such as cartridge paper. An important advantage over some adhesives is its delayed sticking time, which means that sprayed papers can be re-positioned if necessary, and you have time to remove any air bubbles that may become trapped.

Spray adhesive is best used in a confined space to prevent the sticky mist settling on surrounding surfaces. To make a spray booth, choose a cardboard carton large enough to comfortably hold the largest piece of paper you are spraying. Place the box on its side and surround it with newspaper. Place the card or paper shape as far inside as possible. To spray, hold the can upright and spray evenly over the surface with a sweeping motion. With a large piece of covering paper, lay it sticky side up and press the paper or card to be covered over it. Smooth to stick, then trim round the shape as necessary. Turn over and smooth the surface flat.

When laminating very small paper shapes, first lightly spray a piece of white paper so that it becomes tacky. Lay the shapes to be sprayed on this – the tackiness will prevent them being blown about by the spray. They can be eased off the white paper with the edge of a craft knife and positioned on the card.

To keep the spray nozzle from blocking, turn the can upside down and press the nozzle until the spray is clear of adhesive.

## ENVELOPES

A beautiful hand-made card looks better if presented in an envelope. Most cards can be adapted to the size of envelope you have available, or you can make your own.

Choose paper to complement your card. Measure the height and width of the card, and add $\frac{1}{4}$in (6mm) to each measurement. Draw a rectangle to these measurements on the paper, allowing sufficient margin to draw the flaps. The side flaps should each be half the width of the card and the top and bottom flaps should each be approximately two-thirds of the height. Fold the side flaps in first, then spread stick adhesive on the edge of the bottom flap. Fold it over the side flaps and stick in place. The top flap can be stuck in the same way, or a colourful sticker can be used instead.

Decorate the envelope if you wish with a motif used on the card: for example small silver bells or a pink heart in one corner. Or make your own sticker for the back, such as a cat cut from black paper for a good luck card, or a mini penguin. Small rubber stamps can also be used to decorate envelopes.

For cards with raised parts, you could make a shallow box with a lid. Reinforce the corners with pieces of corrugated card or polystyrene.

## GIFT TAGS

An attractively wrapped gift will be enhanced with a specially made gift tag. If you are using giftwrap, laminate a piece of this to a small rectangular card folded in half. Punch a hole near the top of the fold and thread with decorative thread or narrow ribbon. Or cut a motif from the giftwrap. Laminate the motif to card, then cut the card to shape and make a hole in one end. Or you could stick the motif to a piece of rectangular card.

With an unusually shaped box, you could cut a piece of plain card to the same shape.

A gift tag to go with a plainly wrapped gift could be more elaborate. Try personalizing tags to fit the recipient's hobby or the contents of the gift; for example, in the form of an artist's palette, a gardening glove, or a snooker table top.

## MAKING YOUR OWN CORD

Cord adds the finishing touch to many parcels and cards, but the colours of commercially available cords is limited. If you make your own with embroidery cotton, you can match your giftwrap exactly or choose toning colours to set off your gift to perfection.

Cut lengths of embroidery cotton 6 times the length of the required cord. The thicker the cord required, the more threads you use. A length or two of silver or gold thread can be added if you want to make a cord with a bit of sparkle. Fold the thread in half and tie all the ends together. Slip the knotted end over a hook, or ask someone to hold it for you. Put a pencil through the loop at the other end and, holding the threads taut, twist the pencil away from you. You will find the easiest way to do this is to hold the threads with the left hand close to the pencil, so that the pencil is supported, and use your right forefinger to spin the pencil. As the twist increases a kink will form. As soon as this happens, hold the twisted threads in the centre with your left hand and take the pencil to the hook, still keeping the twisted thread taut.

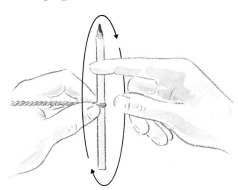

Spin the pencil with your right forefinger

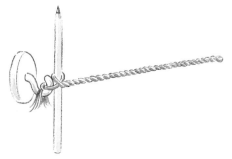

Release the tension from the centre and the threads will twist together

Now, gradually move your left hand from the centre towards the hook and as the tension is released, each half of the twisted threads will twist together evenly.

Slip the end from the hook and take out the pencil. Make a tassel at this end by making a knot 1–2in (2.5–5cm) from the end. Cut off the original knot and loop evenly and unravel the ends to the knot just tied.

## PLEATING GIFTWRAP
Add some pleats to your giftwrap for a professional looking finish. It is advisable to practise first on a few sheets of scrap paper.

First work out how much paper you need by wrapping it loosely around the

gift. For pleats running along the length of the parcel, add extra to the length of the paper. For pleats that wrap around the parcel, add extra to the width.

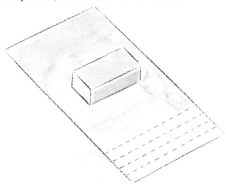

For pleats running along the length of the parcel add extra to the length of the paper

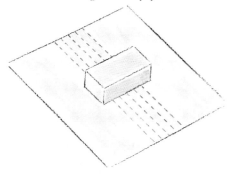

For pleats running around the parcel, add extra to the width of the paper

### Lengthways pleats
Lay the paper flat with the wrong side facing up and one short edge towards you. Fold the bottom edge over by the

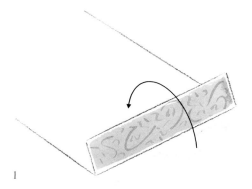

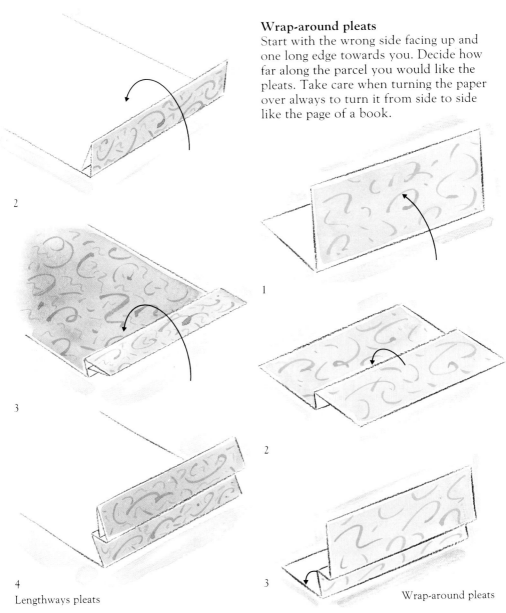

## Wrap-around pleats

Start with the wrong side facing up and one long edge towards you. Decide how far along the parcel you would like the pleats. Take care when turning the paper over always to turn it from side to side like the page of a book.

Lengthways pleats

Wrap-around pleats

width of one pleat (1). Fold the same width over again (2). Turn the sheet over and make a fold half the width of one pleat (3). Turn the sheet over and make a fold the width of one pleat (4). Repeat steps (3) and (4) until you have the required number of pleats. Secure the pleats with pieces of sticky tape across the back.

Make a fold away from you towards the middle of the paper (1). Open out the fold and turn the paper over. Lift the first fold and make a second fold half the width of one pleat from the first fold (2). Turn the paper over and make a third fold the width of one pleat from the second fold (3). Repeat steps (2) and (3) until you have the required number of pleats. Secure the pleats with pieces of sticky tape across the back.

## Using the pleated wrapping

For a neat parcel, fold under both short sides of the giftwrap (unless one end is already pleated). Wrap it around the gift and overlap and stick the short sides on the top with double-sided sticky tape.

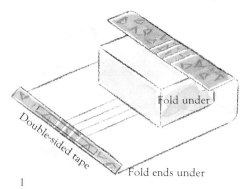

Wrapping the parcel

Fold down the top flap at the ends. Fold in the side flaps, then fold up the bottom flap and secure with double-sided sticky tape.

## RIBBONS AND BOWS

There are a number of types of ribbons which are especially good for making decorative bows. Gift tie ribbon sticks to itself when moistened and is perfect for making all kinds of bows and rosettes. Paper ribbon comes in a tightly twisted rope and, when unfurled, can be used to make big, flamboyant bows. Ribbon with a fine wire edge is ideal for bending into any shape.

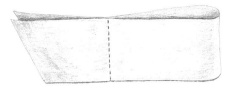

Sew the ribbon together across the width. Cut the ends off diagonally.

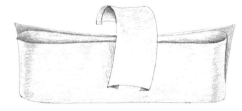

Fold a short piece of ribbon, wrap it round the bow's waist.

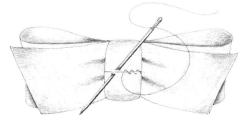

Sew the ribbon ends together on the back of the bow.

## Tailored bow

These are made with gift tie or woven acetate ribbons. Either sew or stick the bow together. Cut ribbon to the desired length, fold in half and sew across the width, slightly less than halfway from the ends. Cut the ends diagonally. Bring the sewn seam to the middle and baste together. Press. Cut another, small piece of ribbon. Fold the edges under. Fold ribbon over the middle of the bow, overlapping at the back. Sew the edges together on the back.

## EMBROIDERY STITCHES

There are hundreds of embroidery stitches to choose from, but the most useful for decorating greetings cards are:

### Straight stitch

Straight stitches can be used singly or to fill in shapes. Bring the needle through at A, insert it at B and bring it through again at C.

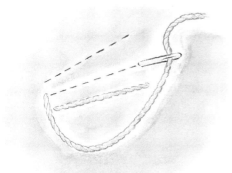

Straight stitch

## Back stitch

This stitch, properly worked, looks like machine stitching. Bring the needle through at A, insert it at B and bring it out at C in front of A.

Back stitch

## French knot

French knots are decorative stitches. Bring the needle through at A, wind the thread round the needle twice, and then insert the point at B, close to A. Pull the thread through so that the knot tightens on the fabric surface.

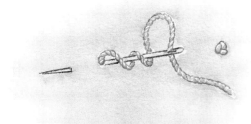

French knot

## Cross stitch

Cross stitch is worked on perforated paper in the same way as on fabric. In the first stage, diagonal stitches are worked from right to left across a certain number of holes. In the second stage, diagonal stitches are worked from left to right to complete the cross stitch.

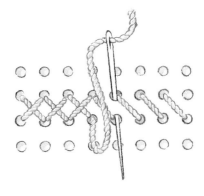

Cross stitch on perforated paper

## Three-quarter cross stitch

The first half of the cross stitch is formed in the usual way. Then the 'quarter' stitch is brought across and down into the central hole. You will find it easier if you first carefully punch a central hole in the perforated paper with a sharp needle.

Three-quarter cross stitch

## Useful addresses

C. M. Offray & Son Ltd,
Fir Tree Place, Church Road, Ashford,
   Middlesex, TW15 2PH
Tel: 0784 247281
Woven satin and gift ribbons
(write for address of nearest stockist)

Paper Magic,
34 Purfield Drive, Wargrave, Berks,
   RG10 8AR
Parchment craft (Pergamano) equipment
(send an SAE for a price list)

Personal Stamp Exchange, US,
Rubber stamps – Star cluster and Vine
   and rose heart were used in the book
For local stockist contact:
Woodware Toys and Gifts,
BV, Unit 2A, Sunnylands Business Park,
   Skipton, N. Yorkshire, BD23 2DE
Tel: 0756 700024